Take up Athletics

Principal contributor:
Peter Warden
BAAB National Athletics Coach

SPRINGFIELD BOOKS LIMITED

Copyright © Springfield Books Limited and White Line Press 1990

ISBN 0 947655 74 3

First published 1990 by
Springfield Books Limited
Springfield House, Norman Road, Denby Dale, Huddersfield HD8 8TH

Edited, designed and produced by
White Line Press
60 Bradford Road, Stanningley, Leeds LS28 6EF

Editors: Noel Whittall and Philip Gardner
Design: Krystyna Hewitt
Diagrams: Chris Oxlade and Steve Beaumont

Printed and bound in Great Britain

This book is copyright under the Berne Convention. All rights are reserved. Apart from any fair dealing for the purposes of private study, research, criticism or review, as permitted under the Copyright, Designs and Patents Act 1988, no part of this publication may be reproduced, stored in a retrieval system, or transmitted in any form or by any means, electronic, electrical, chemical, mechanical, optical, photocopying, recording or otherwise, without the prior written permission of the copyright owner. Enquiries should be addressed to the Publishers.

Photographic credits
Cover photograph: Split Second
Supersport: 6, 11, 13, 17, 18, 23, 26, 28, 30, 32, 34, 39, 42, 45, 46(b), 47, 49, 50, 52(t), 55, 56, 59(t), 61
Noel Whittall: 15, 16, 24, 25, 27, 37, 43
All other photographs by the author.

Acknowledgements
Our thanks to the athletes featured in many of the instructional photographs: Emma Binns, Glen Reddington, Ian Simpson, Louise Stuart and Paul Wray, and to coach Mike Morley.

Contents

1 Introduction — 7
The early days — 7

2 Starting in athletics — 9
The first steps — 9
Give them all a try! — 10
Safety and health — 10
Coaches — 11
Diet — 11
Drugs — 12
Smoking — 12
Clothing — 12
Footwear — 12

3 Elements of training — 14
Not too much too soon — 14
The five Ss — 14

4 Sprinting — 17
The sprint distances — 17
Special equipment — 17
Starting — 18
The sprinting action — 21
Sprint drills — 21
Sprint rules — 22

5 Hurdling — 23
Crossing the hurdle — 23
Learning to hurdle — 25
Isolation drills — 26
400-metre hurdles — 26
Hurdling rules — 28

6 Endurance events — 29
Techniques and training — 29
The steeplechase — 30
The marathon — 32
Race walking — 32

7 The jumps	**34**
LONG JUMP AND TRIPLE JUMP	34
The essential rules	35
Safety	36
Long-jump technique	36
Triple-jump technique	38
HIGH JUMP	40
The scissors	40
The flop	41
Failed jumps	43
POLE VAULT	44
Technique	45
Learning to pole vault	47
Failed vaults	48
Competition rules for high jump and pole vault	49
8 The throws	**50**
Safety pointers	50
THE SHOT	51
The essential rules	51
Technique	52
THE DISCUS	54
The essential rules	55
Technique	55
THE JAVELIN	58
The essential rules	58
Technique	58
THE HAMMER	61
The essential rules	62
Technique	62
Useful addresses	**64**
Great Britain	64
Overseas	64
International	64

Introduction

Take up Athletics will help you to decide which events appeal to you, and how to learn the basic techniques of the ones you choose. We cover only individual track and field events, so relays, road running and cross-country have been left out. In all cases the events covered are those recognised internationally for amateur competition. Throughout this book, only the most basic rules of competition are given. For the full rules, you will need the handbook of your national governing body or the IAAF.

Athletics is really a whole family of sports. Its two main branches are *track* (running) and *field* (jumping and throwing). Within each branch are many different events — see Table 1.

Table 1: athletic events

Track	Field	Combined
Sprinting	High jump	*Women's events*
Hurdling	Pole vault	Pentathlon (100 m hurdles,
Middle-distance	Long jump	shot put, high jump, long
Steeplechase	Triple jump	jump, 800 m)
Long-distance	Discus	Heptathlon (pentathlon +
Marathon	Hammer	200 m, javelin)
Cross-country	Javelin	
Race walking	Shot put	*Men's event*
Road running		Decathlon (100 m, long jump,
Relay (team event)		shot put, high jump, 400 m, 110 m, hurdles, discus, pole vault, javelin, 1500 m)

The early days

Athletic contests have taken place since the days of pre-history. The ancient Greeks have given us many of the expressions we take for granted in modern sport, and we have them to thank for the original Olympic Games, first recorded in 776 BC.

Sprinting is one of the simplest and oldest of the athletics events. It dates back to the original Olympics, in which the chief event was the *stade*, a straight sprint the length of the stadium (192 m).

These ancient sprint races were started from starting-blocks in the form of grooves cut into a block of marble which ran the width of the stadium. The athletes ran naked on hard-baked earth, and runners who made a false-start were whipped!

The ancient Olympics also included middle-distance races, a type of long jump, and throwing events in the form of the discus and javelin.

The marathon takes its name from Greece, but was not originally a sporting event: it commemorates the run of a soldier named Pheidippides. In 490 BC he ran the 35 kilometres from Marathon to Athens carrying news of the Greek victory over the Persians, but as soon as he had announced the victory to the Athenian elders, he collapsed and died.

After the fall of the Roman Empire, little was heard of organised athletics again until about two hundred years ago. In the eighteenth century, sprint races were often organised between servants of the nobility, for the purpose of betting. By the nineteenth century these races had become very popular, and the runners were almost all male professionals. At about this time, amateurs were becoming active too, and many of the events we know today began to take shape.

The first modern Olympics were held in Athens in 1896, and since then progress has been steady. Athletics is now one of the major branches of sporting achievement throughout the world.

Women's athletics was very slow to develop, and has really only come to life in the twentieth century. In ancient Greece women were not even allowed to spectate at athletic events, and in modern times no national associations for women's athletics were founded until 1917. The first international competition was held in 1921. In the Olympics, track and field events for women started in 1928. Today, however, women's athletics is of equal significance with men's.

Measurements
In the mid-1970s, official world records for races run over distances measured in yards ceased to be recognised, and since then metric units have been used almost exclusively throughout athletics. Nowadays the mile and the marathon are the only events which are not run over true metric distances.

2
Starting in athletics

There is enormous variety in athletics: it covers the explosive power of the shot-put, the long steady endurance of the marathon, the gymnastics of the pole-vault and the excitement of the mile. There really is something for everyone!

Athletics is an individual sport in which athlete competes against athlete for personal satisfaction and the thrill of winning. However, first and foremost athletics must be *fun*: if you are not enjoying your athletics, you will not be getting the best out of the sport.

The first steps

First contact your nearest athletics club. If you have problems finding one, you can enquire at your local public library or write to your national governing body. In Great Britain this is the Amateur Athletic Association (AAA), the Women's Amateur Athletic Association (WAAA) or the British Amateur Athletic Board (BAAB) — see page 64 for the addresses. Outside the UK, the International Amateur Athletic Federation (IAAF) will help you to contact your own national governing body.

Before you take the big step of actually joining a club, have a good look at it and ask yourself the following questions:

- Does the club cover a wide range of events?
- Is there a happy atmosphere?
- Are there coaches for most events?
- Is there a special group for newcomers and juniors?
- Do you feel that the club wants *you* as a member, or are they just recruiting to keep the numbers up?

If the answer to more than one question is *no*, then you should probably look elsewhere.

Give them all a try!

Once you have become a member of the club, do not let yourself be pushed too soon into one particular event. At first you should try out many events, and only then decide which you wish to specialise in. You may find that you prefer an event that you had not previously considered.

Age groups
Most events may be altered to suit the age of competitors: lower hurdles are used; lighter implements are thrown; shorter distances run. It is not possible to list all the variations in a book of this size, but it is important for athletes, coaches and parents to be aware of the differences and to ensure that young people do not attempt unsuitable tasks.

The age groups are usually defined as in Table 2:

Table 2 Age groups

Females	Males	Age range
Minors	Colts	11–12 years
Girls	Boys	13–14 years
Intermediates	Youths	15–16 years
Juniors	Juniors	17–19 years

If your age falls within the limits for a particular group at midnight on 31 August, that is your group for the whole of that calendar year. However, juniors have to be under 20 at midnight on 31 December in the calendar year in question.

Safety and health

If you keep to the rules and use basic common sense, athletics is not a dangerous activity. However, if you do not keep your wits about you, or misuse the equipment, you can be seriously injured. There are obvious dangers in events such as the javelin and discus, and these will be dealt with in the appropriate sections. The following points apply at all times, both on the practice field and in the arena:

- Don't fool about when others are training.
- Take extra care when wearing spikes.
- Look both ways before crossing the track.
- Always warm up thoroughly before beginning exercise or competition, and warm down afterwards.

- Juniors should not take part in weight-training or resistance exercises. These can have a damaging effect if used before the age of about seventeen, when the bone structure becomes fully developed.

Coaches

All athletics clubs have coaches, who are there to help you. Make sure your coach holds a qualification from the national governing body; a good coach will not let you train too hard or too soon.

In a good club, with effective coaching and a little talent of your own, you should have a long and enjoyable athletics career. The most important word is *enjoyable*.

Right from the start of your athletics career, always take advantage of skilled coaching whenever you have the chance.

Diet

You should eat a normal balanced and varied diet which will provide everything your body needs. Teenagers should avoid special diets; in some cases they can be positively dangerous.

Many young athletes have become anorexic through excessive dieting in the hope of running faster, and this can have very bad long-term effects. If you are substantially overweight, take the obvious steps such as avoiding double portions of chips and big fried meals, but don't starve yourself: losing too much will not help at all. Your body-weight will come down naturally as you gradually increase the amount of training that you do. When you have stopped growing, at about the age of 20, you can begin to think about a diet specifically planned for peak athletic performance, but talk to someone knowledgeable about it first.

Drugs

In the past some athletes have used drugs to try to enhance their performance. This is exceedingly dangerous to health, as well as being against the rules of sport and morally wrong. Don't do it!

There may be times when you have to take drugs because of an illness, but be cautious. Even simple medicines which can be bought over the chemist's counter can contain drugs that are forbidden by the rules of athletics. For example, some cold cures contain the banned substance *pseudo-ephedrine*. If you might be tested, and have been taking any medication for whatever reason, declare it to the medical team *before the meeting starts*. If possible, get a note from your doctor.

For example, a surprising number of successful athletes are affected by asthma, and many use an inhaler such as Intal to keep the condition under control. However, the active substances in asthma inhalers are on the list of banned drugs, so must be declared in advance.

Smoking

Don't. If you do, *stop!*

No athlete at the very top level smokes. Smoking damages your health, and will stop you reaching your full potential as an athlete by reducing your aerobic fitness.

Clothing

There is a wide variety of athletics clothing on the market. There is very little to choose in quality between the various brands available, and provided the kit fits well it is unimportant whose logo is on the clothing. The essentials are vest, shorts, T-shirt, sweat shirt, socks, tracksuit and possibly a waterproof suit. Women may prefer to wear a sports bra. You should always turn out in clean kit, so you will need at least two sets of everything except the tracksuit and waterproofs.

Footwear

Trainers
All athletes need a pair of trainers ("flats") which fit well, have a good stable heel and cushion the feet effectively. Until you are sure that you are going to stick with the sport and have decided which event is for you, specialised shoes are not necessary.

Spikes

Spiked shoes ("spikes") are used for competition because their grip is much better, but don't rush into buying them. On modern synthetic tracks the majority of training can be done in flats. In fact, doing so will often protect your legs against stress-related injuries such as shin splints.

There are almost as many patterns of spikes as there are different events. For example, runners generally use spikes in the sole only, whereas javelin throwers have them in both sole and heel. The spikes themselves are replaceable, so that you can choose the length to suit the surface.

Training shoes with rubber soles are suitable for most early activities. Here a young athlete learns the basics of javelin technique. She is wearing very simple sportswear which nevertheleless allows complete freedom of movement, while the coach is comfortable in T-shirt and tracksuit trousers.

3
Elements of training

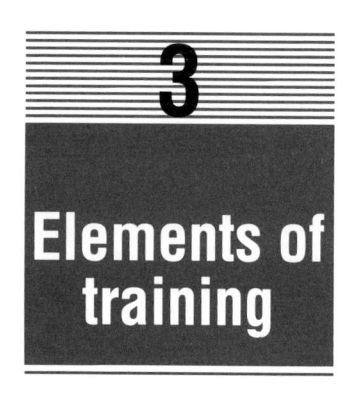

Not too much too soon

When you first begin to take a serious interest in athletics, you naturally want to begin training. Good, but take it gently! Athletes do not reach their full potential until their early twenties or even later, so there is no point in rushing if you still have some years to go. You should first concentrate on developing the *skills* of the sport alongside basic fitness training: later you can benefit from more intensive fitness training.

The best approach is to give yourself a foundation period that can last up to four years depending on how old you are when you start. From small beginnings of, say, two or three fun-sessions per week, you can build up over the years until you train as often as you like. This progressive approach should ensure that you stay injury-free and eventually realise your full potential.

The five Ss

In sport there are five basic elements — the five Ss. All athletics training should contain all five:

- Speed
- Strength
- Stamina
- Suppleness
- Skill

Speed

Speed, particularly speed of limb movement, is essential to *all* athletics events. Explosive speed, sometimes called *power*, is most important in the sprints, hurdles, jumps and throws.

Speed endurance is what gives the ability to maintain fast limb-speeds for a long time — vital for good performances in the 400 m, 400 m hurdles, 800 m and 1,500 m events.

Pure speed is slightly less important for long-distance runners, but even they need speed for a finishing sprint as well as stamina.

Strength

Strength is sometimes defined as the ability to exert *force*; it is vital in the power events — sprints, hurdles, jumps and throws.

Young athletes should start building strength by using exercises in which only their own body-weight gives resistance. Once the bone structure is fully developed, in the late teens, weight training may be safely used — but not before.

Strength training can be made interesting and satisfying by doing it in the form of circuit training. This means performing a series of different exercises arranged in a circuit. A typical circuit might involve sit-ups, step-ups onto a bench, press-ups, twenty-pace shuttle sprints, squat-thrusts and star-jumps. You might start by doing each exercise ten times, and three laps of the whole circuit. As your fitness improves you build up both the number of repetitions and the number of circuits. Circuit training is ideal for endurance athletes for whom weight training is not recommended.

Right: *the press-up from the knees is especially suitable for very young athletes.*

Below left: *sit-ups*

Below right: *squat-thrusts*

Stamina

Stamina, or endurance, is the ability to keep going. *Aerobic endurance* is what keeps you going at steady speeds for a very long period of time. It is dependent on how efficiently your heart and lungs keep your muscles supplied with oxygen. Good aerobic performance is essential for distance runners.

Anaerobic performance arises from a different energy system, which enables the muscles to provide very high power by using the fuel stored within them, without oxygen. It lasts for a relatively short time, but plays an important part in the explosive power events.

Young athletes should develop aerobic endurance before improving anaerobic performance.

Suppleness

Suppleness is often referred to as *mobility*. Good joint mobility is needed in all athletic events, and can be developed through careful training. Young people usually have good mobility which they gradually lose as they get older. Start to do mobility exercises (such as gentle stretching) when you first take up athletics, because it is far easier to keep the mobility that you have than to try to regain it once lost.

Stretching exercises like these should be done progressively, without any violent movements or "bouncing".

Skill

Training for skill varies from event to event: some are highly technical, and need to be taught and then practised very intensively. However, skill alone does not win events — you must develop the correct blend of all the Ss.

Planning your training

The training time you give to each of the Ss will depend on the event, the season, and your age. Your training programme should be carefully planned with the help of your coach.

4

Sprinting

The sprint distances

In modern track athletics, the outdoor sprint distances are 100 metres, 200 metres and 400 metres, plus 60 metres indoors.

Hayley Clements of Kent leading in a schoolgirls' 200 m sprint.

The main skills of sprinting are good starting and the correct sprinting action. The longer sprints are specialised events for older, more experienced athletes; you need good coaching before tackling them.

Girls under the age of 15 are not allowed to compete in 400 m races, and it is sensible for boys to wait until that age too, before taking on the "long sprint".

Special equipment

Serious sprinters need spiked running shoes. The length of spike should be chosen to suit the running surface: you generally need shorter spikes on all-weather tracks than on grass.

Once you decide to specialise in sprinting, you will also need a set of starting blocks. These are adjusted to suit you, and are pegged to the surface of the track just before each race. You don't need to buy starting blocks at first, since most athletics tracks will provide them, but you may decide to buy your own later.

Starting

You need quite a lot of strength to benefit from a crouch start, so newcomers up to the age of about twelve should begin with a standing start and then learn the crouch start, at first without blocks.

The standing start

Place your stronger leg forward, with the toe of your front foot just up to the starting line. The other foot should be about one shin-length back.

The arm opposite your front leg should be forward. For example, if your left foot is at the front, your forward arm should be the right one.

To start your sprint, lean forward slightly and drive your rear knee forwards with a high, fast and hard action. At the same time the elbow of your front arm should drive back as your rear arm drives forwards. The result will be a very fast stride down the track: keep the first stride short and sharp.

The crouch start

- *On your marks*
  Place the toe of your front foot exactly the length of your foot behind the starting line. Kneel so that your rear knee is level with the toe of your front foot. Place your fingers just up to the line, but not touching it, with your hands shoulder-width apart.

- *Set*
  From the "on your marks" position, raise your hips so that they are higher than your shoulders. Your shoulders will move slightly ahead of your hands, but take care that they do not move off-centre. To ensure that your head stays in the right position, look at a point about one metre down the track. Don't try to look at the finish.

- *Go*
  The first part of your body to move when the gun goes off is the arm opposite your rear leg. In the illustrations this is the left arm. This arm is punched forward and up as the elbow of the other arm is driven backwards. You should concentrate on getting a good range of arm movement as you pull

the rear knee forward. This knee should come forward fast and high, before the foot is driven vigorously down to the ground.

Louise Stuart demonstrates the "on your marks" position. Her fingers are forming a high bridge and her shoulders are almost directly over her hands.

The "set" position. The angle of the front knee is approximately 90 degrees; that of the rear knee is approximately 120 degrees.

"Go". There has been a strong upward drive from the rear leg, and the front leg is fully extended. The arm action is really vigorous, the body stays low, and the head remains aligned.

Shirley Strong on the mark using starting blocks

Starting on a bend

The very high acceleration at the start of a sprint race is easiest to attain in a straight line. However, the 200 m and 400 m sprints start on a bend, and instead of starting at right-angles to the line, your position must be slightly altered to enable you to run straight for the first few strides. This also means that your left hand must be placed a few inches back from the normal starting line. If you are using starting blocks, they too must be positioned at a slight angle to the starting line.

Placing the starting blocks on a curve; the tapes show the effect of the offset.

Which foot forward?

In all sprint starts, your stronger leg should be the one that is forward when you are in position on the line. Your stronger leg is usually the one which you automatically choose to take off from when you jump.

The sprinting action

Sprinting demands the correct action and a large range of movement.

Figure 1 shows all the features of a good sprinting action:

- The runner's head is aligned with his body and he is looking down the track.
- The rear elbow is high.
- The front thigh has a good high lift.
- The rear leg is fully extended.
- He is achieving a good "split" between the legs.
- The toe of the front foot is cocked upwards.

This type of sprinting action often develops naturally, but can be learned if you know what you are aiming at.

Figure 1
A good sprinting action

Sprint drills

The most common method of improving sprinting technique is by using *sprint drills*. These exercises break down the action into its component parts, work on each part, and then put them back together again into the full technique. To gain the full benefit from sprint drills, you need to be supervised by a good coach who can see the parts of your technique that need improving. You must work hard too!

Typical drills include the walking sprint (an exaggerated sprinting action done at walking pace), flicking the heels while running steadily, prancing, running fast while raising the knees very high, and a variety of skipping exercises. These drills develop the muscles you need for sprinting and encourage joint flexibility.

Sprint rules

- Starting blocks must be rigid, and made without springs which could help the sprinter.

- Before the start, competitors must not touch the start line or the ground in front of it with their hands or feet.

- When a crouch start is used, *both* hands must be in contact with the ground.

- It is a false start if any competitor leaves his or her mark before the gun is fired.

- You are only allowed to make one false start in any race; if you make a second one, you will be disqualified.

- In races run in lanes, you must keep in your own lane from start to finish.

- The finishing positions of the competitors are judged according to the order in which their torsos cross the line.

A close finish in a schoolboys' 100 m

5

Hurdling

"Hurdling is sprinting over barriers." This is an oversimplification, but it sums up the essence of hurdling. The emphasis must be on speed, both between the barriers and over the barriers. The technique of crossing a hurdle must be learned so thoroughly that it can be done fast and without conscious thought.

The distances of sprint hurdles are 100 m for women and 110 m for men. Under-13s run 80 m, while the indoor distance for all ages is 60 m. The 400 m hurdles is rather more than a sprint, and is an event for the older, more mature runner. The rules do not allow athletes under the age of fifteen to compete in the 400 m hurdles.

The 300 m hurdles is for intermediate girls only.

Great hurdling style, with straight leading legs and good split positions

Crossing the hurdle

As you approach the hurdle, drive the knee of your *leading leg* towards the top of it, at the same time as your opposite shoulder and arm. Your lower leg and foot will then automatically flick out and over the hurdle. Do not attempt to get the leg over the hurdle in a straight line. As soon as the heel is over the top, pull it back down and under you and straighten the leg.

As you clear the hurdle, your *trailing leg* should be left behind as long as possible and then brought round flat and wide. Once clear, do not let this leg drop down to the ground: keep pulling it round in front of you so that the knee is high; this can give you a long powerful first stride off the hurdle.

You will find that your arms will co-ordinate with your legs without you having to think about them.

The two key words in hurdling are:

- *knees* because it is the knees that lead the hurdle action,

- and *attack* because you must attack the hurdle aggressively.

Glen Reddington two metres from the hurdle, and just about to take off. His body is upright, and he is looking straight down the track. His right knee and left arm lead the action.

Over the hurdle: for maximum efficiency Glen's front leg should be straighter, with the toe cocked upwards more.

Good style on landing: the trailing leg has come round sideways and is continuing high in front of the body. The landing leg is straight, with the heel off the ground. The runner is now in a good sprinting position, with a slightly exaggerated knee lift. He is in balance, and has been looking straight down the track throughout the jump.

Learning to hurdle

Don't start by trying to clear a full-size hurdle as best you can. There is a good chance that you will injure yourself, and you will soon become fed up. With hurdling, you start low and work up. To set the practice hurdles at the right spacing to teach you the action, get your coach or a friend to watch you sprinting over about 40 metres and lay out six canes as shown in Figure 2, at 3-pace intervals.

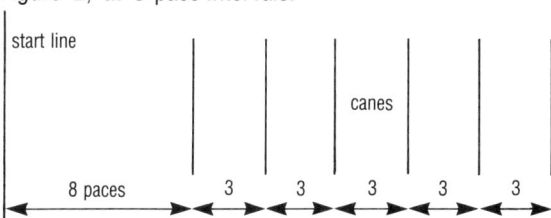

Figure 2 Spacing the canes for hurdling practice

Now make a note of the spacings, and replace the canes with adjustable hurdles set low so that you can gradually increase the height of the barriers during the next few sessions. It will be very easy to clear the barriers at first, but you will be getting used to the all-important skill of meeting them without really having to think about it. When the hurdles are raised to about 500 mm, you will have to begin concentrating on bringing the trailing knee round sideways.

Once you have developed a sound hurdling technique, the distance between the practice hurdles is gradually increased until you are covering the height and spacing that the race rules require for your age and sex.

Isolation drills

Once you have learned the basic hurdle-crossing technique, you will need to work on improving it and making it faster. The usual way of doing this is by using isolation drills. In these, only one leg passes over the hurdle, the other one going around the side. This allows you to concentrate on improving your technique one leg at a time. Isolation drills need to be tailored for you, and you need a coach to comment on your good and bad points.

400-metre hurdles

The 400 m hurdles is a tough event, but is really no more difficult than many others, provided that you are fit before you tackle it and build up to it steadily with adequate training. Do not try out the 400 m hurdles as a full event just to see what it is like or "for the points".

400 m problems

- You will be hurdling on a bend. If you lead with your right leg, it is quite easy to let the left leg trail around the inside of the hurdle. Doing this can lead to disqualification.

- Setting the right stride pattern is much harder than it might appear. The hurdles are 35 m apart, and you have to know how many strides to take between them. However, as fatigue increases towards the end of the race, your stride length shortens, and the stride pattern has to be changed. The point where this happens is called "change down", and you must train to perfect this.

Hurdle safety

- Always jump a hurdle from the side towards which its feet are pointing, *never* from the other direction.

Glen demonstrates how a hurdle tilts easily when approached from the correct side: too many athletes have been injured through casually jumping from the other direction and failing.

- Place the balance weights as close as possible to the uprights of the hurdles, so that they will tilt with the minimum of pressure.

- Do not use hurdles whose tops have sharp edges or splits. These are a common cause of cuts to the legs.

- Check that nobody else is using the hurdles before moving them.

- Remember that hurdles are for hurdling, not for leaning on or hanging your tracksuit on!

Hurdling rules

- All hurdle races are run in lanes, and each competitor must stay in his or her lane throughout.
- In races where the hurdles comply with international specifications for size and the amount of force needed to knock them over, the athletes may knock down any number accidentally without being disqualified. If the hurdles can be knocked down with less than the specified force, athletes who knock down three or more are disqualified.
- When clearing a hurdle, a competitor who trails a foot or leg around it, below the level of the top, will be disqualified.
- Any athlete who *deliberately* knocks down a hurdle will be disqualified.

800 metres: the shortest of the middle-distance events

6

Endurance events

This is a very wide category which includes all the running events from 800 metres to the marathon, the steeplechase, and race walking. Endurance events are usually divided into several main categories:

- Middle distance: 800 m; 1500 m; mile
- Long distance: 3000 m; 5000 m; 10,000 m; steeplechase
- Marathon
- Race walking
- Road running
- Cross-country

Most athletes look upon cross-country or road running as ways of getting competition in the winter and as excellent training methods. However, some runners specialise in them and never race on the track. Older athletes often compete in a wide range of endurance races.

Techniques and training

The middle-distance events do not demand as much technical expertise as, say, the jumps or throws. Each person runs in a slightly different way, but provided your natural running action is efficient, there will be no need to change anything. For example, your arms should move backwards and forwards in a relaxed manner with little movement across your body.

You should wait until your later teens before tackling endurance events longer than the mile. Concentrate on the shorter distances such as the 800 m and 1500 m at first, only increasing the distances as you get older.

Don't attempt to run big training distances as a junior. While you are going through your foundation period, simply enjoy general athletics activity. Three sessions a week are enough, working mostly on mobility exercises and body-weight strength exercises, with a little endurance running. There should also be some work done on speed and skill.

Obviously, if you are going to fit all this into three sessions per week you *cannot* and *should not* be out "clocking up the miles" at every possible opportunity.

Roadwork warning
Preparing for the long-distance events demands high training mileages. Naturally, much of this running tends to be done on hard road surfaces, which often leads to severe and recurring lower-leg injuries. This danger is greatest for young athletes, who should keep road mileage to the minimum and do as much of their running as possible on grass.

The steeplechase

The steeplechase is an interesting and demanding event. During the 3000 metres, 35 barriers have to be crossed, seven of them having the additional hazard of a shallow water-filled trough 3.6 metres wide on the landing side. The barriers are the same height as the men's 400 m hurdles but are solid. The running element of steeplechasing is the same as in all the other long-distance events, but you should spend some of your training time with the 400 m hurdlers in order to improve your technique and speed.

The water jump in the steeplechase is tackled once in each lap.

The water jump

The dry barriers are normally hurdled without touching, but the water jump is a special problem which comes up on every lap of the race. You should aim to cross this using the "one foot wet" technique. In this, you approach the barrier in the usual way, but instead of clearing it, your lead foot should land on top of it. Bend the leg and keep your body low over the barrier, pushing off with the lead foot as you pass over it. Your rear foot should be brought forward rapidly to become the landing foot, and this is the only one that gets wet. A good "split" in the air is needed here.

Figure 3 How to clear the water jump

Endurance safety

- Never run within two hours of finishing a heavy meal.

- Always obey the local rules of track discipline.

- Always wear bright reflective clothing when running on the roads at night.

- Where possible, run on the pavement. If you must use the road, always run facing oncoming traffic.

- Do not run in badly worn shoes. This is a false economy which may damage your feet permanently.

- Try not to run alone. If you must, tell someone where you are going and how long you intend to be.

The marathon

Marathons and other ultra-long-distance events are not suitable for novice runners, and in your determination to finish you may do damage to your body which could affect your whole running career. Keep to middle-distance, and perhaps the 3000 m to 10,000 m long-distance events, until you are a really mature runner.

Race walking

The IAAF definition of race walking is:

"A progression by steps so taken that unbroken contact with the ground is maintained. During the period of each step, the advancing foot of the walker must make contact with the ground before the rear foot leaves the ground. The supporting leg must be straightened (i.e. not bent at the knee) for at least one moment when in the vertical upright position."

Incorrect walking technique will not only mean that you will be disqualified, but can also result in quite severe long-term injury: so you need tuition from a qualified coach before taking up race walking.

Good hip mobility is essential for successful race walkers.

Race walking takes place on both the track and the roads. On the track the recognised competition distances range from 1500 m to 50 km; there are also one-hour and two-hour races. On the road, competition distances are from 5 km to 50 km. For women, the maxima are one hour or 10 km on the track, and 20 km on the roads.

Only two races are included in the Olympic Games — the 20 km and 50 km for men.

Race-walk essentials

- Each pace must include a *double-support phase*, when both feet are in contact with the ground.

Figure 4 Double-support phase: the heel of the front foot lands first; the front leg is straight; the rear foot is pushing away with the toes and the arms are nicely controlled, being bent at the elbows without any hunching of the shoulders.

- From the double-support phase, your rear foot should be brought forward, keeping it as near to the ground as possible.
- All your weight is now supported on one leg, which should stay straight for as long as possible.
- Each foot, when in contact with the ground, should point straight forward and not be splayed either in or out.

Using your hips

Good hip mobility is essential for race walkers. With each pace, your hips should be displaced slightly to the side. This stops your body rising and falling, which wastes time and may cause your rear foot to lift off early. Your hips should also swing forward with your front leg in order to give a slightly longer stride. This is called "gain".

7

The jumps

There are four jumping events in modern athletics: the long jump, the triple jump, the high jump and the pole vault.

LONG JUMP AND TRIPLE JUMP

The long jump requires a combination of speed and strength, but is not a complicated event. Beginners start by using the simplest technique, called the stride jump. More advanced techniques such as the "hitch kick", "hang" and "sail" give the athlete more control over the landing position.

Judy Simpson in full flight

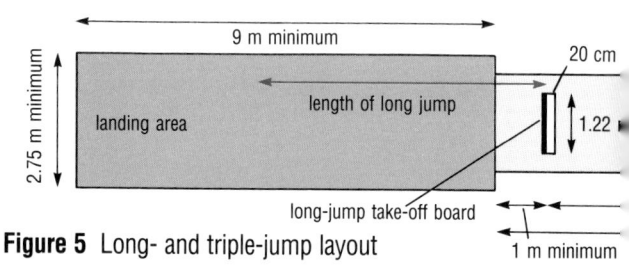

Figure 5 Long- and triple-jump layout

Triple jumping started in Ireland during the nineteenth century, as a standing hop, skip and jump. It has undergone a number of changes before turning into the modern event with its running start.

Until 1990, international triple-jump events were held for men only.

The competition order is decided by drawing lots. Each contestant makes three attempts, and the best eight are allowed another three. Only your best attempt counts, unless there is a tie.

The essential rules

In the long jump and triple jump, your distance is measured from the *take-off line*, which is the front edge of the take-off board, to the nearest point in the landing pit that your body touches. You should therefore pace out your run-up and practise it so that your take-off foot hits the board quite close to the front. To help with this, you are allowed to place markers alongside the runway, but not on it. You can use any length of run-up you wish.

A strip of clay or Plasticine abuts the front edge of the board, so that if you overstep, your toe will leave a mark.

The landing area should be of damp raked sand, and level with the take-off board.

Your jump will fail if:

- you touch the ground beyond the take-off line with any part of your body, except when landing.

- you take off from outside the ends of the board.

- while landing, you touch the ground outside the landing area nearer to the take-off line than the break in the sand to which the measurement of the jump would have been made.

- you walk back through the landing area, having completed the jump.

- you use any form of somersaulting.

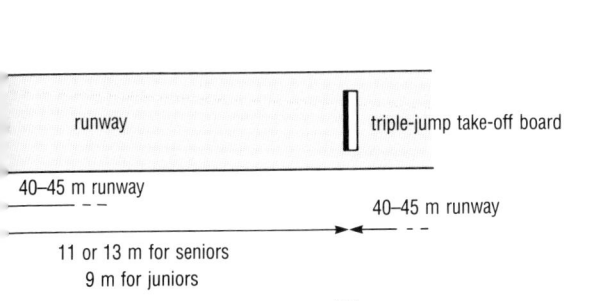

| runway | triple-jump take-off board |

40–45 m runway

40–45 m runway

11 or 13 m for seniors
9 m for juniors

Safety

- Before jumping into a sand pit, spend a little time digging and raking the sand in case there are hard objects such as bricks hidden just under the surface.

- Rake the pit regularly during your jumping session.

- When you are not using the rake, keep it well out of the way.

- On cinder or grass run-ups, ensure that there are no hollows or lumps — particularly between the triple-jump board and the pit. Hollows can be filled with sand from the pit.

Long-jump technique

Run-up

When you are learning the long jump, use an approach run of between 10 and 12 strides from a standing start. Pace this out by working back from the take-off board. This relatively short run will ensure that you are in control at take-off, and also not too tired to jump. Your first strides do not have to be as fast as when sprinting, and your running style should be more upright: speed is built gradually at first.

During the last few strides you must prepare for take-off: pick your knees up higher and increase the speed of your legs. The next-to-last stride should be slightly longer than the others.

Take-off

Regardless of the technique you use for the rest of the jump, the take-off is the same:

- Plant the take-off foot slightly ahead of your body with a vigorous down-and-back action.

- Keep your hips high, with an upright body position.

- To assist in getting height at take-off, your free, non-jumping leg is brought upwards, with the knee bent.

Figure 6 The stride-jump action

- Use your arms in a normal running manner and keep your head in line with your body — don't let it tilt backwards.

Flight and landing

Once you are in the air you cannot propel yourself forwards any more, and all the movements you make are to keep your balance and prepare for landing. You must aim to maintain the stride phase, with your body upright, for as long as possible. Then, just before landing, bring your take-off leg forward to join the free leg, and bend your trunk forwards too. The object is to get your legs out in front of your body in what is known as "leg-shoot", so that they hit the landing pit as far ahead as possible. You have to get your trunk forwards at the end of the jump so that you don't "sit back" on landing and lose the valuable distance that your feet have gained.

Ian Simpson during a training session. His style is perfect in this jump, but if you look carefully at the first picture, you will see that he has overstepped the take-off board.

Triple-jump technique

All three parts of the triple jump tend to be of similar length. The first jump is a hop from which you have to land with the same foot that you used for take-off; the second is a step onto the *other* foot, from which you launch into the final element which is like a normal long-jump.

For the jump to be legal you are only permitted the two single-foot contacts at the end of the hop and step. If another part of you touches the ground at any time between the first take-off and the final landing, the attempt is disqualified.

Each phase of the triple jump should be higher than the previous one; you should feel as if you are jumping uphill.

> **Footwear**
> It is important that you have the right kind of shoes for the triple jump. Both spikes and trainers need thick shock-absorbent heels, and must fit really well.

Run-up
Use quite a short run-up while you are learning, increasing to between 14 and 18 strides once you have mastered the basic technique. Experienced adults usually use 17 to 21 strides. The running action is similar to that of the long jump, but with a little more control.

The hop
The take-off for the hop is very much like the long-jump take-off, but with rather less emphasis on height. Just as in the long jump, you should drive the non-jumping knee high.

Figure 7 The triple-jump action

During the hop, you must bring the take-off leg forwards fast, so you can land on it. The landing from both the hop and the step must be very "active": the leg must be working out, back and down to meet the ground with the foot flat. Don't land with your leg stiff, or you won't be able to launch from it into the next phase.

The step
You take off into the step at a slightly steeper angle than for the hop. Hold the split for as long as possible before pushing the landing leg ahead of your body and clawing it down and back for the landing.

The jump
Good height is essential in the jump phase. Beginners should use the simple stride jump with a good leg-shoot, as described for long jumping. Once you have become completely familiar with the whole triple-jump technique, you can begin to experiment with more advanced styles for the final jump.

Triple jump — the hop phase. This is the first part of the sequence; triple jumpers aim to increase the ground clearance during the step and jump which follow.

HIGH JUMP

Modern high jumping requires a combination of speed, strength and agility. It is an advantage to be tall, although there are some world-class performers who are only slightly above average height.

High jumping was popular among professionals in the nineteenth century, but they usually approached the rope or bar like a hurdler. Then the "scissors" style was developed: in this the jumper approaches the bar at an angle and "scissors" his legs over it, one after the other. Around 1910, the "western roll" appeared, in which the jumper crossed the bar more or less on his side. Thirty years later came the "straddle", a stomach-downward crossing.

The technique used by present-day high jumpers is called the "flop", invented by Dick Fosbury of the USA. In the flop, you go over the bar on your back, with head and shoulders leading.

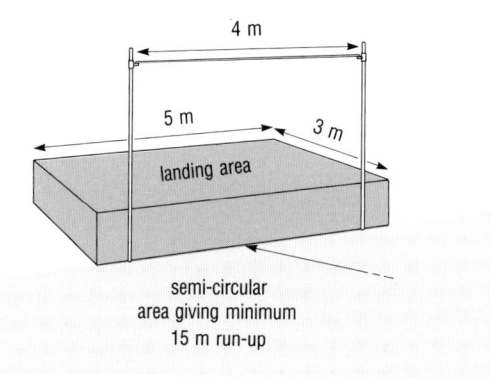

Figure 8 High-jump layout

You start by learning the scissors, then the flop. The run-up and take-off can be the same for both.

The scissors

Run-up

The most important parts of a high jump are done on the ground: the run-up and the take-off. In flop jumping, the run-up is always curved, so if you use a curved run-up for scissors, you will be able to convert easily later on.

Modern jumpers use a run-up that is shaped like a letter "J". The first part of the run-up is straight, but the last few strides curve in towards the bar. Beginners use between 7 and 9 strides, of which the last 4 or 5 curve.

If you are running fast enough, you will naturally lean in towards the curve, like a cyclist going round a bend. This lean away from the bar will become very important when you convert from the scissors to the flop.

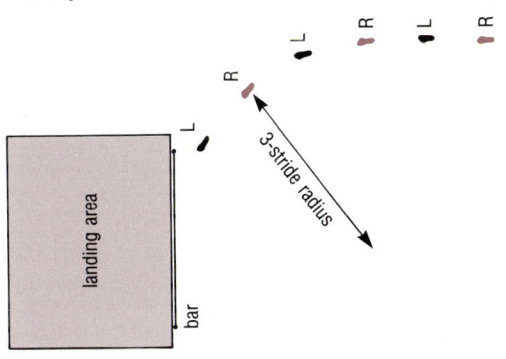

Figure 9 Curved run-up

Figure 9 shows a typical curved run-up for a jumper using a left-foot take-off. Note how you take off very near to the upright, not at the centre of the bar. This ensures that you will land in the middle of the landing area.

You are allowed to place markers on the ground to help in your run-up, and you may also place a handkerchief, or something similar, on the bar as a sighting guide.

Take-off

Facing the bar at an angle, you take off from the foot furthest away from the bar, so right-footed jumpers approach from the left and vice versa.

The flop

Your run-up is just the same as for the scissors: as you take off, use a strong upward swing of the non-jumping knee and the arm nearest the bar. You change your body's inward lean on the curved run to an upright position at take-off, but the combination of the curved approach and the upward drive of your arm and leg will make you twist in the air so that you cross the bar on your back (see photo on page 42).

You should not try to twist by turning your foot away from the bar or by swinging your non-jumping leg across your body. Your take-off foot must be in line with its leg, and the drive from your knee should be straight upwards.

Once your bottom has cleared the bar, lift your legs vigorously to stop them knocking the bar off. At the same time bring your head forward so that your chin is on your chest. This will help to lift your legs, and it ensures that you land safely on your shoulders.

Because you might land on your neck, the importance of performing the flop only onto a *safe* landing area cannot be stressed too highly.

High-jump safety

- You must only attempt the flop into a properly-constructed built-up foam landing area. Always check the landing padding thoroughly before jumping.

- If you do not have a good built-up foam landing area, the only safe high-jump technique is the scissors.

- Always tie the foam modules together when making up the landing area.

- Check at regular intervals that the modules have not moved.

- *Never* jump onto a landing area without walking all over it first to check that it is safe.

- Use an elastic bar when training.

Approaching the bar: the jumper's body is just twisting so that she will clear it on her back.

The body is over ...

... the legs are raised rapidly and the back curved to ensure that the feet don't catch the bar.

Failed jumps

High-jump rules require you to take off from one foot, but there is no restriction on how you cross the bar. An attempt fails if:

- in the course of a jump, you knock the bar off the pegs.
- you take off from both feet.
- any part of your body touches the ground beyond the plane of the uprights without first clearing the bar. This includes the landing area and the ground outside the uprights.

The competition rules for high jump are discussed together with those for pole vault on page 49.

POLE VAULT

Pole vaulting is probably the most exciting of all the events. Pole vaulters need the skill of the gymnast, the power of the long jumper, the speed of the sprinter, and tremendous courage of their own.

Pole vaulting looks difficult, but if properly taught it is quite simple. Most youngsters can master the basic fundamentals of run-up, plant, take-off and swing in one session; after that it is merely a question of application.

At first, bamboo, aluminium and steel poles were used, but in the late 1950s flexible glass-fibre poles were introduced. The end of the pole is planted into a metal slide-box.

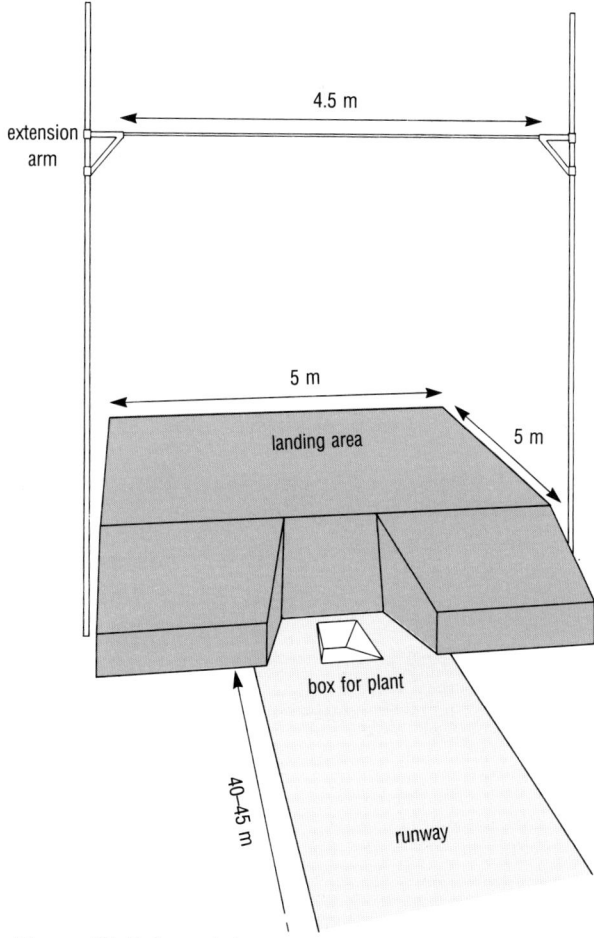

Figure 10 Pole-vault layout

Technique

Run-up

Pole vaulters make an approach run of between 13 and 21 strides. The older and faster the athlete, the longer the run-up. You must learn to run fast while keeping the pole under control.

The pole is carried with the front hand on top of the pole and the rear one underneath. The rear hand holds the pole with a palm-out grip. A right-handed vaulter will start the run with his right (rear) hand close to his right hip pocket and his left hand just below chest height. The hands should be a little more than shoulder-width apart. In the first part of the run-up the pole is carried almost vertically.

The plant

As the run progresses, you steadily bring the pole down to a near-horizontal position. The plant is made during the last three strides of the run-up by lowering the pole rapidly: you move your rear hand from the hip-pocket area to a position as high as possible over your head. This should be completed before your take-off foot lands for the final time.

Take-off

This is very like the long jump take-off. The free or non-jumping leg must be driven high with the thigh parallel to the ground. You must think about jumping *long* in order to begin to bend the pole.

Paul Wray shows the pole vault take-off position.

Swing

As you gain height, you swing on the pole while still holding the "free" leg high.

The rock-back

The rock-back enables you to get your feet above the top of the pole as it straightens out. It is essential to have a good bend on the pole and to keep your body well back from it. Both legs are brought rapidly up to your chest. Don't attempt the rock-back until you have mastered the basic technique of pole vaulting.

Pierre Quinon of France, in the full rock-back position. The pole is fully curved, his knees are being pulled in towards his chest, and his body is well back from the pole.

The pull
As the pole straightens, you pull yourself towards it and straighten your legs so that they are almost in line with the pole.

The push and the clearance
The final few inches are gained by pushing yourself upwards from the now straight pole, and over the bar.

Paul Phelps has completed the push, and his body is resuming the legs-down position.

Learning to pole vault

Pole vaulting, especially at the very beginning, should not be done without supervision.

You can get the feel of the event by practising low vaults into a sand pit. Do not use a bar, or any equipment other then a safe pole — at this stage you are concerned with getting the overall feel of running with the pole and *swinging* on it. Position your top hand about your stretch-height from the bottom of the pole, and hold it as described on page 45. Take a few fast strides, plant the end of the pole in the sand, and take off, concentrating on distance.

Figure 11 Learning to pole vault

Figure 11 shows the technique. Note how you stay behind the pole and *swing*. Lift your legs high — level with your chest if you can — and keep hold of the pole as you prepare to land.

You can grip the pole higher as you gain confidence; the higher the grip, the longer the vault! However, the higher the grip, the faster the run-up needed too. If you are right-handed, swing past the right-hand side of the pole; left-handers swing past the left side. You can have lots of fun mastering the basics like this before getting a skilled coach and progressing to vaulting for height.

Pole-vault safety

- All the safety measures for high-jump landing areas (see page 42) apply equally to the pole vault.
- Take care of the pole. Do not drop it, stand on it, or subject it to sharp knocks or extremes of temperature. Always store it in its case.
- Be taught by a coach, using proper equipment.

Failed vaults

A vault fails if:

- you knock the bar off the pegs.
- you touch the ground, including the landing area beyond the vertical plane of the upper part of the slide box, with any part of your body or with your pole, without first clearing the bar.
- you place your lower hand above the upper one or move your upper hand higher up the pole, either at the moment of take-off or at any time after leaving the ground. This rules out any attempt to climb the pole.

If your pole breaks during a vault it is not classed as a failure.

Competition rules for high jump and pole vault

In high jump and pole vault, the jumping order is decided by drawing lots. A minimum height is set to open the competition, and *you* decide when to start jumping. You can make up to three attempts at each height, but do not have to jump at any particular height. Three consecutive failures, regardless of height, disqualify you from further participation except in the case of a jump-off to decide a first-place tie. In other ties, the decision is given to the tied jumper with the fewest attempts; if that doesn't settle it, the jumper with the fewest fails gets precedence.

The bar is raised one centimetre each time for high jump, and eight centimetres for pole vault.

A fine clearance: Andy Ashurst (England) is in perfect control as he releases the pole for the final descent.

8
The throws

For the sake of simplicity, all the instructions are given for right-handed throwers. Left-handers simply read *left* for *right*.

The competition order is decided by drawing lots. Each contestant makes three attempts, and the best eight are allowed another three. Only your best attempt counts, unless there is a tie.

Safety pointers

All the implements used in the throws are potentially lethal, so never forget these basic safety rules:

- Never throw towards anyone.
- Keep your eye on the thrower at all times.
- Always carry javelins upright.

Javelins must always be held and carried upright.

- When not using a javelin, leave it sticking upright in the ground.
- Before lifting the javelin up to your shoulder, have a quick look to see that no one is standing behind you.
- Always walk to fetch your implement — don't run.
- Always *carry* your implement back to the place from which you are to throw — never throw it back.
- Never throw a hammer or discus without using a safety cage.
- When throwing in a group, keep to a routine in which everyone throws and waits, then everyone fetches.
- Treat the implements with respect — never fool around with them.

THE SHOT

The essential rules

Modern rules require the shot to be "put" with one hand directly from the shoulder; you are not allowed to take it behind the line of your shoulders. You must start from a stationary position inside the seven-foot circle, and not leave the circle until the shot has landed, when you leave by the *rear*. Your feet may touch the inside of the stop board, but not its top.

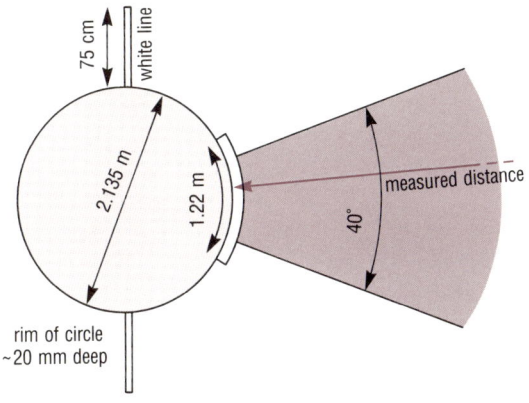

Figure 12 Shot-put area

The weight of the shot varies according to age group (from 3.25 kg for colts, to 7.26 kg for senior men).

The shot is popular with both men and women. This is Judy Oakes in action.

Technique

Two techniques are used today — *linear* and *rotational*. Beginners should start with the linear style, which is explained here.

Holding the shot

If your grip is incorrect, the shot will not go far, no matter how good the rest of your technique: the shot should be held at the base of your first three fingers, with your thumb and little finger adding support. It is then placed under the corner of the jaw, and your elbow held high.

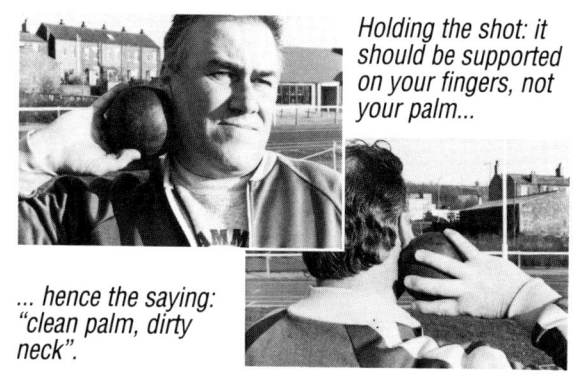

Holding the shot: it should be supported on your fingers, not your palm...

... hence the saying: "clean palm, dirty neck".

Standing throw (front-facing start)

The standing-throw position is fundamental to shot putting, whatever technique you eventually adopt. Your feet should be parallel and pointing in the direction of the throw. For your first attempts, take up the starting position, place the shot correctly against your neck, and put it without using any leg or body movement. Keep your elbow high throughout the throw.

The basic standing throw (front-facing)

Standing throw (rear-facing start)

This is the position upon which more advanced shot-putting technique is based. Begin by standing sideways in the circle, with your shoulders turned around square to the rear (see Figures 13 and 14). Your left toe should be opposite your right instep, with the left foot slightly back from the direction of the throw. Your chin, right knee and right toe should be in a vertical line — the "chin-knee-toe" position.

Start the throw by pushing with your right leg so that your hips move forward over your front foot. Your shoulders should follow your hips round, with your arm coming in "fast and last". Remember to keep your elbow high throughout the throw, and keep the left side of your body rigid and "tall" as your arm does its work. Complete the action by following through.

Figure 13 The standing throw (rear-facing start)

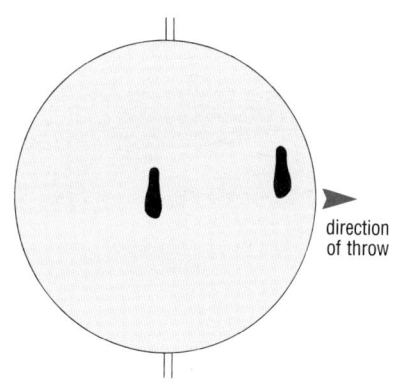

Figure 14 Placing your feet correctly for the standing throw

Movement across the circle

Once you are getting consistent distances from the standing throw, you can begin to use the full diameter of the circle. Try starting from the back and taking a couple of sideways-shuffling half-steps before throwing. This will add distance, provided that you go through the standing-throw position accurately to make your throw. Once you have got the feel of moving in the circle, get a good coach to help develop your technique.

THE DISCUS

The discus is a solid disc, thicker at the centre than at the rim. It is thrown from a 2.5 m circle. The weight of the discus for competition varies from 0.75 kg to 2 kg, according to age and sex.

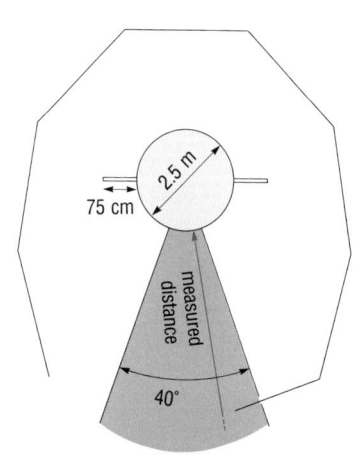

Figure 15 Discus-throwing area

Kevin Horne at the moment of releasing the discus. Look carefully at the picture and compare it with Figure 16 on page 56 to see just how the discus should leave the thrower's hand.

The essential rules

- You must start from a stationary position inside the circle.
- You must leave the circle by the rear, *after* your discus has landed.
- The discus must land in the designated sector.

Technique

Grip

You hold the discus with your hand spread out on the top and the first joints of your fingers just over the edge. The discus should not be gripped tightly. Test your grip by swinging the discus vertically, and then horizontally: you will probably have to use your other hand to steady it at the front of the horizontal swing.

The correct discus grip demonstrated by Jeanette Picton

Standing throw (front-facing start)
Get the feel of the discus with a few standing throws. For these you stand with your body and feet facing in the direction of the throw. Start with the discus near your left shoulder, with your right hand on top and some support from the left hand underneath. Then, using your right hand only, make a full backswing and release the discus partway through the forward swing.

Spin
The discus must spin in the air if it is to travel any distance. You impart the spin with your forefinger on release, producing a clockwise spin when the discus is viewed from above. It is wrong to release the discus from your little finger.

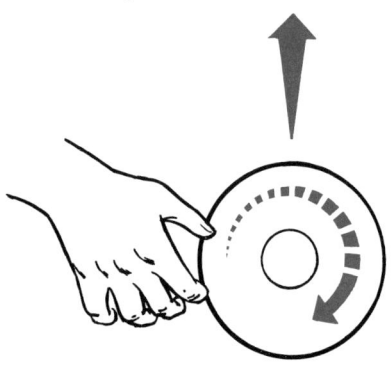

Figure 16 Releasing the discus

Standing throw (rear-facing start)

The starting position is very similar to the "chin-knee-toe" position used in the shot (page 53), but here you are allowed to take the missile as far back as you like. This position is essential to good throwing technique, and must be mastered before moving on to the next stage.

Place your feet as for the shot put, but with the front foot placed slightly further back. The discus should be held behind your right hip, with your arm almost straight.

The movement from this starting position is begun by your right leg pushing your hips forward and round. The shoulder follows, and your arm comes in "fast and last" with a slinging movement. The whole action is like unwinding a tightly coiled spring. Try to keep your hips ahead of your shoulders and your shoulders ahead of your arm as your body unwinds. Your hand must be kept on top of the discus at all times. Try to feel a long swinging movement of the arm, with the discus being kept as far away from your body as possible. Don't forget to follow through!

Your experience with the standing throw will show you that the angle at which the discus is released has a great effect on the distance it travels.

Figure 17 The standing throw

Movement across the circle

Once you have mastered the standing throw, you add speed and distance by getting your body moving effectively in the circle. The most commonly used method of doing this today is known as "running rotation". Briefly, the object is to make a running turn which ends up with a step in which your right foot lands near the centre of the circle, and the left foot near to the rim at the front; your whole body should be twisted ahead of the discus. You continue the rotation and release the discus with a powerful slinging motion. To develop an effective throwing style, you will need guidance from a coach on the field.

The Javelin

The spear has always been an important weapon until modern warfare, and javelin-throwing as a sport grew out of this. The modern event is strictly regulated, especially the throwing technique. The javelin is the only throwing event to use a straight runway, not a circle.

The essential rules

The design of the javelin is strictly specified. Weights of between 400 g and 800 g are used, according to age and sex.

The javelin must land point-first within the boundaries of the landing area, but does not have to stick in the ground. The distance of the throw is measured back to the scratch line from the place where the point first touched the ground.

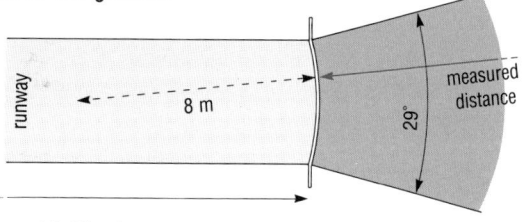

Figure 18 The javelin-throwing area

Technique

The javelin has to be thrown from above the upper part of your throwing arm or shoulder, and at no time may you turn your back on the throw until the javelin has landed. These requirements prohibit the unorthodox and dangerous styles which have been attempted in the past.

Choosing your grip

There are three popular ways of holding the javelin: try all of them before choosing the one you find most comfortable. Your trial throws need only be very short — start with the javelin above your head and stab it into the ground a few metres ahead of you.

In all three methods, part of the grip is on the shaft behind the binding (this stops the hand sliding down the javelin), and the javelin lies *along* the palm of the hand and not across it. Both to comply with the rules and to produce spin on release, some of your fingers must grip the binding.

Fatima Whitbread showing the perfect combination of style, effort and commitment

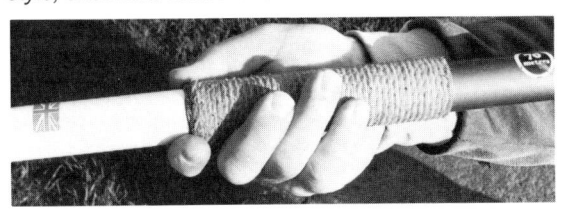

The normal grip

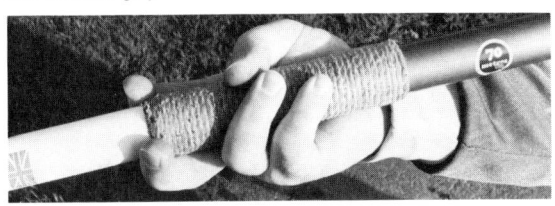

The "V" (or claw) grip

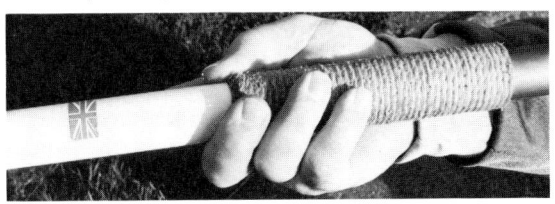

The second-finger-and-thumb grip

Standing throw

The starting position is very similar to that of the discus and shot. The chin, knee and toe should be in a vertical line, but the body is not turned as far round as in the previous two events. The throwing arm should be straight but not locked rigid, and the javelin should point upwards at about 45 degrees.

To make the throw, think of your whole body as a bow which you tension and then release. The right leg should drive the right hip forward. The right shoulder follows, and then the arm comes in "fast and last". Your left side should be almost rigid throughout, and you end the action with a good follow-through.

Figure 19 The standing-throw sequence

Three-stride throw

Begin facing square-on to the direction of the throw, with the javelin held above your right shoulder, and both feet together. Take the javelin back into the throwing position, with your throwing arm straight out behind you. Now stride forward with your left foot, followed by a long, fast, high stride with your right foot — this is called the *cross-over* phase. Finally, push your left foot well forward to put yourself into the throwing position, and *throw*.

Figure 20 The three-stride throw

Once you have mastered the three-stride throw, it is easy to extend your run-up. Do this by adding two strides at a time. The length of the runway used in competition will be at least 30 metres, so you will be able to use as many strides as you need. As with all the other throws, you need a good coach to observe your technique and advise you on improving it.

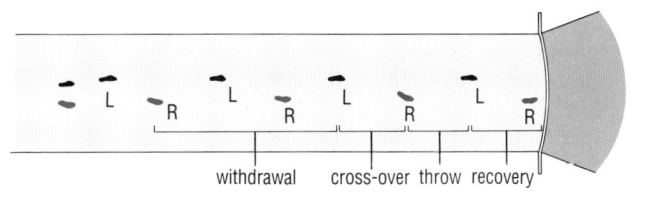

Figure 21 The foot placings shown here are for a seven-stride approach (a good intermediate approach). As you are not allowed to pass beyond the line, the javelin has to be thrown from a full stride behind it, so that you can stop without stepping over it.

THE HAMMER

Hammers with a rigid handle are still used in the Scottish Highland Games, but the implement thrown in international competition consists of a spherical weight attached to a length of flexible wire, with a metal handle at the other end. The hammer is thrown from a circle slightly smaller than the discus circle.

David Smith in the hammer circle

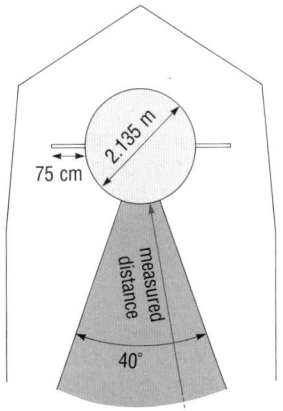

Figure 22 The hammer-throwing area

The essential rules

Although the weights vary according to age, the length of the full-size competition hammer must be between 117.5 cm and 121.5 cm.

- You must start from a stationary position inside the circle, but the hammer head may rest outside if you wish.

- Once you have started to throw, you must not touch the ground outside the circle or the top of the circle rim.

- The hammer head is allowed to touch the ground during a throw, but if it does, you must not stop and start the throw again.

- You leave the circle via the rear half, *after* the hammer has landed.

Technique

From a standing start, most club athletes revolve three times, steadily accelerating the hammer, until finally releasing it at an upward angle of approximately 45 degrees when it has reached maximum speed. Some experts manage to make four complete turns, but this is very difficult to do without stepping outside the throwing circle. The hammer has to land within the area shown in Figure 22.

Young throwers should use a light hammer and concentrate on mastering the technique. All throwers will learn more easily if they start with the short hammer and progress to the medium length before attempting to throw the full-sized one. Without qualified supervision, you should not attempt to throw the hammer with anything more than a standing throw.

Grip
Hold the hammer handle in your left hand so that the grip lies along the base of your fingers; then place your right hand so that the fingers overlap those of your left hand.

Forming your grip, shown here on a short practice hammer

Basic standing throw
Stand facing away from the direction of throw with your feet about shoulder-width apart and the hammer low down on your right side. Swing the hammer forward and sling it over your left shoulder, releasing it so that it is thrown directly behind you. At the finish, your arms should be outstretched high over your left shoulder.

Once the basic standing throw has been mastered with the short hammer, try the same movement with a medium-length hammer, if one is available. If you have to progress straight to a full-length hammer, ensure that it is a light one.

Pendulum throw
The next stage is to extend the standing throw by adding a pendulum swing. Starting with the hammer low on your left, swing it up to eye-level and then down to the starting position on your right. It will go a little further behind you before being swung up and over your left shoulder for the throw.

Keep your feet about hip-width apart: as you accelerate the hammer your hips must be ahead of your shoulders and your shoulders ahead of your hands. Your chin, right knee and right toe should form a vertical line. Concentrate on keeping your left arm straight throughout. You should have the feeling of giving a long pull to the hammer.

Turning in the circle
By learning the pendulum throw, you will have begun to get a feel for hammer-throwing. If you wish to progress further, you must learn how to move in the circle. *You don't immediately try to do three complete turns with a heavy hammer!* Use the lightest hammer you can find, and be guided by a coach. The principle that a straight left arm keeps the long pull going applies all the time. Once you can do one full turn and release the hammer accurately, you build up to the three, or even four, turns you need to produce competitive distances.

Useful addresses

Great Britain

British Amateur Athletic Board
Amateur Athletic Association
Women's Amateur Athletic
  Association
Edgbaston House
3 Duchess Place
Hagley Road
Edgbaston
Birmingham
B16 8NM

Northern Ireland AAA
House of Sport
Upper Malone Road
Belfast
BT9 5LA

Scottish AAA
Caledonia House
South Gyle
Edinburgh
EH12 9DQ

Welsh AAA
Morfa Stadium
Upper Bank
Landore
Swansea
West Glamorgan
SA1 7DF

Overseas

Athletics Australia
PO Box 254
Moonee Ponds
3039 Victoria
Australia

The Canadian Track and Field
  Association
1600 James Naismith Drive
Gloucester
Ontario
K1B 5N4
Canada

New Zealand AAA
PO Box 741
Wellington
New Zealand

The Athletics Congress of the USA
  Inc.
PO Box 120
Indianapolis
Indiana 46206/0120
USA

International

International Amateur Athletic Federation (IAAF)
3 Hans Crescent
Knightsbridge
London
SW1X 0LN